—— J e n n y   M o s l e y '

CIRCLE TI...

HANDBOOK

...for the Moppy stories

Helping children to understand their emotions

Illustrations by Gerald Scarfe from the stories by Jane Asher

Positive Press

Published 2005 by:

Positive Press Ltd
28A Gloucester Road
Trowbridge
BA14 0AA
Telephone: 01225 719204
Fax: 01225 712187
E-mail: positivepress@jennymosley.co.uk
Website: www.circle-time.co.uk

ISBN 1-9048660-9-3

Printed by:
Heron Press
19-24 White Hays North
West Wilts Trading Estate
Westbury
Wiltshire
BA13 4JT

Contents

How to use this book

This handbook offers practical ideas for developing children's emotional intelligence in circle time and provides extension activities.

The 'boundaried' space of circle time allows the children in your class to explore and manage their feelings in a safe environment, where everyone is valued. Circle time is an opportunity for genuine listening, promoting positive relationships and empathy.

Although the material in this handbook can be used freely as stand-alone activities, it has been designed to complement the Moppy storybooks by Jane Asher and Gerald Scarfe. Every time Moppy experiences a different emotion, he changes colour. Children will be more comfortable talking about their feelings when they use Moppy's experiences as a metaphor for their own emotions.

Six key feelings are explored in this handbook:

Happy   Sad   Angry   Calm   Excited   Afraid

Each feeling is introduced with a script for a circle time session that follows the Five Steps to Quality Circle Time *(see page 4-5)*. The teacher's 'script' is presented in italics. Each session is followed with a set of extension activities to build on your work in circle time.

How circle time works

The aim of Quality Circle Time is to nurture children's social and emotional growth and strengthen their self-esteem. Although each meeting is planned and directed by the adult circle time leader, its aim is to encourage children to interact with confidence because each individual is given the opportunity to contribute to the group and feels supported by other members. This helps everyone to work as a team that celebrates difference in others and respects their values and beliefs. Regular circle meetings help children to become emotionally strengthened, socially confident and able to cope with the stresses and strains of life.

These outcomes can only happen if an atmosphere of trust is established from the very beginning of each meeting. For this reason, each session begins with two introductory phases that are designed to help the children into the correct frame of mind. Key issues can then be investigated until the time comes to wind the meeting down. Two further phases lighten the mood and ensure that everyone feels safe, comfortable and ready for the next part of the school day.

Each circle time session begins with everyone seated to form a circle and facing the centre.

STEP 1 Meeting up – playing a game

Begin each meeting with a fun warm-up activity or opening game. This helps the children to relax and feel the pleasure of being together. It often involves a game that requires the children to change places so that they find themselves sitting with classmates who are not their usual companions. This gives them the opportunity to make new friends and helps to build group identity.

These games need to be played quickly and need not take more than a few minutes. For some classes, it is best not to start with a highly energetic game: a more relaxing activity like 'Pass a thumbs-up' may be chosen.

STEP 2 Warming up – breaking the silence

This step is designed to remind children that they all have the right to speak and the responsibility of listening during circle time. The circle leader makes this as straightforward as possible by giving the group the beginning of a sentence, for example, 'My favourite colour is…' Each child repeats this beginning and completes it with a word of their choice. This is called a 'round'.

A 'speaking object' is used to show whose turn it is to speak. Whoever is holding it has the right to speak uninterrupted. The speaking object is then passed to the next person. This object needs to be small enough to fit into little hands: a painted wooden egg is often used. A small fluffy toy works well, or an object can be chosen to fit in with topic work.

Holding the speaking object does not oblige anyone to speak and any child who does not wish to do so may say 'pass' and hand it on. However, some children often say 'pass' because they don't have the confidence or they are testing out the teacher. It is possible, the day before circle time, to tell children what the round is going to be and give them a chance to prepare what they want to say on a small card.

Children who have not got a sentence ready can be gently coached by the teacher before circle time. Very young children can be shy and often it is a good idea to sit in a small circle, before the big circle time, with a puppet who chats to children about what will happen in circle time and who will offer to speak for the child if he is shy.

STEP 3 Opening up – exploring issues that concern the class

Now that the children are relaxed and have practised speaking and listening, they are ready to tackle the most challenging phase of the meeting. This is sometimes called 'open forum' because it is an opportunity to express opinions and discuss important issues.

This middle phase is vital for encouraging children to develop a belief in their ability to make responsible choices and decisions. Problem-solving skills can be rehearsed and targets can be agreed. It is important that children remember to raise their hands (or make a 'thumbs-up') before speaking; speak one at a time and listen to each other. Many practitioners teach children to use the following prompts:

Child: '*I need help because…*'

Teacher/peers: '*Would it help if I…?*' or '*Would it help if you…?*'

Alternatively, this phase may be used to investigate and practise specific skills. Some children are not ready to take responsibility for their actions or to have a spotlight of attention shone on them. It is advisable for some teachers to explore the use of metaphor to help children discuss difficult issues. Stories, role-play, games, puppets, the dressing-up box and other props can be used to help children to sensitively explore other problems, concerns, hopes or fears.

STEP 4 Cheering up – celebrating the positive

Before a circle time session finishes it is important to move the children away from the issues of concern that were investigated in the middle phase of the meeting. The 'cheering up' phase is used to celebrate the group's successes and strengths and give praise and thanks to one another. This can be immediate praise for the work they have done in the meeting or can include a more general celebration of recent school accomplishments.

You could also use this step to allow children to cheer up by learning something new. Children can go into the middle of the circle and teach other children a new playground game. In short, this step makes people feel more competent, happy and positive.

STEP 5 Calming down – bridging children forward

It is crucial that children experience quiet and calm before they leave the classroom to go to another activity. This activity is called 'bridging': you are helping a child experience a closing ritual so that the transition to the next part of their day is smooth and successful. Some teachers play a very calm game like 'pass the tambourine without a sound'. Alternatively, a guided visualisation, 'mood' music, or a rain-stick can be used to introduce simple meditation techniques to your group. In this way you touch the children's imagination thereby strengthening their inner core. What they learn through this step is that they have sufficient inner resources to calm down and make themselves feel happy.

Allow around 45 minutes for a session involving all of the five steps. You can select activities from the five steps for a shorter version, but NEVER end on 'Opening up' (step 3). It is essential that you provide a bridge from your work and discussion in this part of your circle time to the rest of the school day.

Introducing Moppy

The green creature let go of the washing line and landed at David's feet.

'My name is Moppy,' it said. 'I jumped down from a star very high up in space. I don't know what to do now.'

'Perhaps you'd like to come to stay with me for a bit,' said David. 'You don't bite or anything, do you?'

'Only food,' answered Moppy. 'And I'd love to stay. You seem very friendly.'

(From Moppy is Angry by Jane Asher and Gerald Scarfe)

I did my useless non-artistic sketches and stood over Gerald while he drew. The antennae – which are a brilliant touch – were entirely his addition, and are an extra way of expressing Moppy's thoughts and feelings.'

When Moppy's emotions are balanced he is green

Moppy is a green fluffy creature from outer space. Every time Moppy experiences a strong emotion, he changes colour…

'I knew I wanted the character to be fluffy, but at the same time not too cute,' says his creator Jane Asher. 'Children can be self-absorbed (mostly because they've not yet learnt that you're supposed to pretend that you're not) and I wanted Moppy to reflect that and also to have a volatile temperament - another childhood attribute. That's why I knew Gerald was the perfect person to illustrate him. He has a soft side which doesn't often get a chance to come through in his work, but I knew he'd give Moppy that tough edge that was so important.

Red = angry

'The story came first, and I had a pretty strong image in my mind of how I wanted Moppy to look.

The use of colour as a metaphor for the emotions also has potential when working with children with special educational needs. Jane Asher is President of the National Autistic Society and explains how a tool that helps children develop awareness of reading other people's moods can be helpful:

Yellow = happy

'With autistic spectrum disorders there can be a great problem with empathising, and in spotting and interpreting an emotion that another person is feeling. Moppy just might be a useful tool in communicating the subtleties of emotion to those that struggle with all kinds of communication. This visualisation of the invisible might be very helpful. Although I originally wrote about Moppy before I was involved with autism, I would be delighted if he were to prove useful in this way.'

Pale green = calm

Blue = sad

6

What is emotional intelligence?

Emotions are the central organising force for all human experience. Our personal and social well-being is dependent upon our ability to master the complexities of what is now known as emotional intelligence. We are not born emotionally intelligent: babies express their feelings dramatically precisely because the pre-frontal lobes of their brains are not 'wired up'. Their emotions are registered and are immediately acted upon because the areas of the brain that are linked to conscious experience of emotion are not yet active. The instinctive feelings that they emote are called the primary emotions – happiness, sadness, interest, surprise, fear and anger.

At about the same time as language areas become active in the brain, infants begin to develop the self-consciousness necessary to become aware of their changing emotional states. They begin to learn how to identify, interpret, manage and control them. The subtle nuances of emotions that adults can feel, name and act upon are cognitive constructs that become more and more sophisticated as we mature. In other words, emotional intelligence is learned and can be taught.

As with any other area of cognitive development, we need to start learning young with simple activities that can be built upon gradually. In the case of emotional intelligence we need to start with an understanding of the primary emotions and apply that knowledge to four vital facets of experience:

- the ability to understand your own emotions
- the ability to express your own emotions
- the ability to regulate your emotions
- the ability to empathise.

Colour as a metaphor for emotion

When we use colour to describe emotion, we are giving children an easily accessible metaphor to explain something that can be difficult for them to put into words in any other way. When we begin to teach the rudiments of colour in art lessons, we begin by identifying the primary colours and proceed to showing how these can be mixed to make an increasingly refined palette of subtle hues. By using colour as a metaphor for emotional states, we can help children to experience an emotional palette in exactly the same way. Every emotion involves a unique combination of the unconscious primary emotions that we feel so strongly.

To use this method during story time you need a colour to signify each emotion. In the Moppy stories, the following emotions are explored and indicated by a colour:

| Happy = yellow | Sad = blue |
| Angry = red | Calm = pale green |

In this handbook, two further emotions are explored:

| Excited = orange | Afraid = white |

You can easily make a strip of card with a section for each colour. Ask the children to colour it in with the appropriate colour for each emotion. They can bring their colour strip to the story corner and point to how they think a character will be feeling at appropriate times in a story, without you needing to interrupt the flow of the tale.

After each story you can develop their understanding by asking what strategies were used to change emotions. For example, how did a character change from blue to yellow?

Why use stories?

Stories show us a range of personalities. They describe how the characters feel and the actions that they take. Each character teaches us something about emotional actions and their consequences. The strong emotions we feel and the predicaments that we face are described and solutions are offered. Stories explain how other people are likely to react to our behaviour and give us a means of understanding our own emotions.

Stories are called 'boundaried space' because they distance the reader/listener from their own immediate lives. Children are able to discuss the behaviour of story characters without feeling the anxiety that they would experience if asked to describe real situations.

We can combine the metaphor of colour and the power of stories and teach emotional intelligence through a blending of the two using the series of Moppy storybooks. Moppy is a furry little alien who changes colour when he experiences a strong emotion. He begins each story as a green ball of fluff. If he gets angry, for example, then Moppy turns red. When he is happy, Moppy is a sunny yellow.

circle time session

The text in italics suggests a script for the circle time leader to follow.

Use the five steps of circle time to explore the emotion of happiness

What you need
- A copy of the book *Moppy is Happy*.
- Something that sparkles.

Moppy is Happy

Moppy is Happy is the first book in the Moppy series, and tells the story of David's first meeting with the little alien.

David sees something flash past his window one night, and goes out to investigate. Hiding in the watering can is Moppy, who has just landed from a distant star...

Both David and Moppy are a little unsure of each other, but with some welcoming words from David they soon become friends.

David's parents aren't too keen on the new visitor at first, but Moppy soon charms Mrs Jones. And then something amazing happens. Because he's feeling happy, Moppy changes colour – to a bright, beaming yellow!

Meeting up

'I am thinking about happiness today.'
'When I am happy, the ends of my mouth go up and I smile.'
'When I am happy, my arms want to move up – like this – and give someone a big hug!'
'When I am happy, my feet want to jump up and dance.'
'Happiness is a very "up" feeling. There are many ways to share the feeling which we can pass round the group.'

- Now give a 'thumbs up' to the child next to you. Let them pass on the gesture, around the circle, until it comes back to you.

Warming up

- Pass a speaking object (see page 4) from child to child. Give each member of the group the opportunity to complete the following sentence, *'I feel happy when…'*

opening up

- Put one hand behind your back and ask the children if they can tell whether you are doing a 'thumbs up' or a 'thumbs down'.

'You can guess, but you don't really know, do you? That's no good! It's the same with happiness or a smile. If you can't see it, you don't know how I am feeling today.
'The best smiles are the ones that we share. That's a very important thing about happiness. Happiness is very "catching" so it works best when it is shared!'

- Read the story *Moppy is Happy*.

'What made Moppy and David happy?
'Yes, they made friends, didn't they? Friendships are another kind of sharing that makes us happy.'

- Ask the children to talk about the things that have made them feel happy.

'Well, we've learned a lot about what makes us happy. Who can think of words that describe how it feels to be happy?'

- Take suggestions from the children and praise their ideas.

happy

Cheering up

- Think of some recent occasions when your group of children have made you feel happy. Perhaps they were working quietly and co-operating well, or performing a wonderful assembly. Smile and tell them about these occasions, involving the children's contributions.

Calming down

- Close the session with a sharing round, passing a sparkly object around the circle.

  'I have a good word for how happiness makes me feel. The word is "sparkly" and I have a sparkly object to show you what I mean. We can all share the happiness!'

- Pass the object to the child next to you and say, 'I give you my happy sparkle so that you can sparkle too.' As they hand on the sparkle they should share a smile.

Extension activities

Use these activities for follow-up sessions with your class. 'Build a happy person' and 'Join the dance' (page 10) are great fun at the end of your circle time meeting.

Activity one – good wishes

- Discuss the following sentence with the children, and then think of different classroom situations where good wishes would be useful.

  'When someone gives me praise and good wishes, I feel happy inside. That means I know that I can give happiness to other people with my good wishes.'

- Ask the children to think of some good-wish statements that they would like to receive and that could be useful in your classroom. Examples might include:

  'Don't worry, you'll get there.'   *'I like you.'*   *'You're a good friend.'*

- Write your good wishes on some star shapes. Fix the stars on to sticks or straws, put them in a jar and let the children create happiness by giving magic wands to one another. If they return them to the jar at the end of the day, the magic wands can be re-used throughout the year.

- Use the star shapes to make a board display. Glue them on to a board and draw or stick a decorated wand beneath each one to make them look like magic wands. The display will remind the children that giving and receiving good wishes makes us happy.

◀ **For the 'good wishes' activity you will need...**

- A selection of star shapes.
- Some straws or light sticks to make wands.
- Tape and glue for fixing.

9

For the 'you're welcome' ▶
activity you will need...

- A poster or book showing 'welcome' written in various languages.
- Pictures or storybooks which illustrate a contrast of welcoming places and hostile places.
- Stickers and materials for decorating certificates.

Activity two – you're welcome

- Tell the children that people like to feel welcome. It makes them feel warm and happy and wanted. Discuss how we can show that we are welcoming with our expression, the way that we move and the way we speak. We can say, 'You're welcome' and make other people smile. We can make our rooms welcoming so that people feel relaxed and happy as they come through the door. Discuss ways in which we can be welcoming towards each other and make every day a happy 'You're welcome!' day.

- Explain to the children that different cultures have different forms of greeting, such as the Japanese bow or the French custom of kissing both sides of the face. Older or more able children may be able to investigate and demonstrate some other greetings. Research how the word 'welcome' looks and sounds in different languages.

- Ask the children to find illustrations in their storybooks that show the contrast between welcoming and hostile places. Discuss the ways artists convey these opposing atmospheres through colour and graphic techniques.

- When the children have focused their minds on how they will make sure that their classroom is always a welcoming place, use reward certificates to thank the ones among them who offer a welcome in the most generous way.

Activity three – build a happy person

- Sit the children in a circle. Explain that we show happiness in many different ways. Suggest a few examples: skipping, punching the air, dancing, laughing, sighing happily.

- Now choose a volunteer – a child who has to demonstrate or suggest a way in which we show happiness. Ask another volunteer to copy the first child's action, and to demonstrate another way of showing happiness. Ask a third child to copy both the actions and to add another of her own. Keep adding volunteers and actions to the list until the volunteer can't remember the order. At this point, she flops to the floor and says, 'I'm so happy, I can't move.' Now it is someone else's turn...

Activity four – join the dance

- Use joyful, happy music for this activity. Latin American samba usually works well. Ask the children to sit down and then choose a confident volunteer who likes to dance.

- Play the music and let the volunteer show the class a dance. When you call 'smile', the volunteer must go to the group, smile and take someone by the hand and bring them to join the dance. Call 'smile' again so that the second child can repeat the invitation. Continue until all the children are dancing. Don't forget to join in yourself!

- Discuss with the children how we can use our bodies in joyful, energetic ways to make us full of happiness. It's a scientific fact!

Activity five – the feelings tree

- Find a small branch which has plenty of twigs to resemble a small tree. Paint it white and plant it in a tin of sand or some clay. You also need some little baskets of plastic eggs in the following colours. Each colour signifies a feeling:

YELLOW =	HAPPY
BLUE =	SAD
RED =	ANGRY
PALE GREEN =	CALM
WHITE =	AFRAID
ORANGE =	EXCITED

- When the children come into class each morning they can choose the coloured egg which expresses their mood. When their name is called in the register, each child replies 'Good morning, Miss, I'm [name colour] today'. They can then hang their egg on the feeling tree. This little ritual informs you of each child's current mood and, if it is negative, you will be able to give children the attention they need to change their egg to a more positive colour.

◀ For the 'feelings tree' activity you will need...

- A small branch with plenty of twigs to make a small tree for display.

- Some white paint for decorating your tree.

- Coloured plastic eggs in a variety of colours: red, pale green, yellow, blue, orange and white. If you can't get hold of plastic eggs, make some oval shapes from coloured card.

Sometimes we are ..

circle time session

The text in italics suggests a script for the circle time leader to follow.

Use the five steps of circle time to explore the emotion of sadness

What you need
- A cloak.
- A goblet.
- A blue shape to symbolise sadness.
- A small bell or triangle.

Moppy is Sad
In this book Moppy comes to terms with the death of a pet.

Moppy meets David at the bus stop and explains that something very worrying is happening at home. When they get back, Mrs Jones explains that the goldfish has died.

Moppy is troubled and wants to spend some time on his own. He thinks that it might be his fault for not looking after the goldfish properly. Nothing seems to make him feel better.

With the help of David, friends and family, Moppy is no longer feeling blue – in more ways than one.

Meeting up
- Ask everybody to stand up. Make eye contact with a child and smile. The child should smile back and sit down. Continue with the action until everyone is seated.

Warming up

'A smile is a friendly expression that makes other people feel happy. There is a word that means the opposite of happy and that word makes us move with heavy steps and look hunched or droopy. I'll show you what I mean…'

- Demonstrate sad body language to the children.
  'Does anyone know the word that means the opposite of happy?'

- Take suggestions from the children and tell them that you are going to talk about that word (sad) today because you have been reading a story about Moppy where he felt sad and blue.

- Using the speaking object (see page 4), ask each child around the circle to complete the sentence 'Sometimes I feel sad when...'

opening up
- Choose a confident child and give him a cloak to wear.

  'May I introduce King/Queen [insert child's name]. Let's see how the King is feeling today.'

- Take the child to the centre of the circle. Ask him to sit down with his knees pulled up to his chin, arms round knees and head down, looking miserable and lonely.

  'What do you notice about the way that the King is sitting?
  'Yes, he is all alone. He is huddled up. He's not looking around. He seems to have lost interest in everything. He's not talking to anyone. How do you think he is feeling?
  'Yes, I agree. He must be feeling sad and lonely.

sad

'I have an idea! I have a special cup in my bag. It's called a cup of kindness. It can do a wonderful thing. I'll show you how it works.

'It's quite easy really. All I have to do is give the King the cup of kindness and say something kind to him. Then he can take a sip.

'Say something kind to the King. Give him the cup and let him take a sip. It doesn't usually work straight away. He might need quite a few sips before he stops feeling sad. Would anyone else like to give the King a sip from the cup of kindness?'

- Help the children to think of kind things that they could say to the King: 'You can come and play with me,' or 'I like your cloak'. When the King has had enough sips from the cup of kindness, ask him to stand up and smile at the group saying, 'I was sad but the cup of kindness has made me happy again'. Now ask the King to walk happily back to his seat.

Cheering up

- You will need a blue shape to symbolise sadness and a bell or musical triangle. Ask the children to pass the shape around the group until you ring the bell. The child who is holding the blue shape at that moment must say, 'When I am sad I like someone to...' (smile at me, do a funny dance, tell a joke and so on.)

- Now say, 'Will anyone do this (insert the cheering activity) for (insert child's name) and make him happy?' Choose someone to do whatever has been requested. Continue to pass the blue shape around.

Calming down

- Reflect on the positive message that everyone can take from the session. Ask the children to breathe calmly and close their eyes.

'Some sadness is very big and takes a long time to go away. But a lot of sadness is caused by little things. Just a few unkind words can make someone feel sad and lonely. Kindness is something magic that can make someone feel quite different. Kindness can take a lot of sadness away and make it disappear. Remember how we can all help people to drink from the cup of kindness every day, instead of feeling lonely inside the cloak of sadness.'

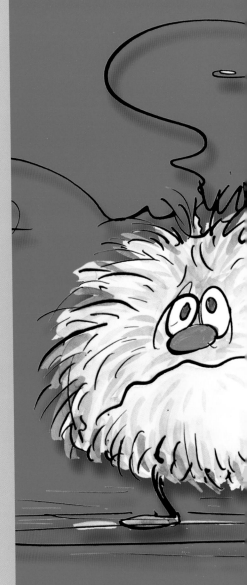

Extension activities

Use these activities for follow-up sessions with your class. 'Turn it around' is a good choice at the end of your circle time meeting.

Activity one – finger play

- This action rhyme reinforces understanding of an act of kindness.

Little Susan, down at the end [Hold up one hand.]
Was sad and lonely without a friend
[Put index finger on lips and make a sad face.]
Friendly Simon looked her way [Put hand above eyes and look around.]
Asking her to come and play [Beckon with crooked finger.]
With his lovely yellow ball [Pretend to catch a ball.]
Sue was happy after all [Point to a big smile.]

Activity two – the queen's medal

For the 'queen's medal' activity you will need... ▶

- A selection of plain badges or small card circles and ribbon to make medals.

- Explain to the children that good friends are people who know how to act – and how not to act – as friends. Good friends can make us happy and bad friends can make us sad.

- Ask the children to tell you the 'dos' and 'don'ts' of a good friendship. If they are stuck you can offer the following suggestions until they understand what you are looking for.

Friends take turns in games.
Friends stand up for each other.
Friends cheer each other up when they are sad.
Friends don't play mean tricks on each other.
Friends don't make fun of one another.

- Invite the children to choose a 'rule of friendship' and design a medal for it. These can be awarded in the classroom to celebrate acts of friendship.

Activity three – the kindness cushion

For the 'kindness cushion' activity you will need... ▶

- A cushion with a soft cover.

- Sewing materials to add a pocket to one side of the cushion.

- Find a cushion with a soft cover and sew a pocket on to one side. Tell the children that this will be their 'kindness cushion' and that anyone who is feeling sad will be able to sit and cuddle the cushion.

- Tell the children that the cushion has a special pocket and that you will be putting secret messages into the pocket. Ask them what kind of messages they would like to find inside the pocket when they are feeling sad. Collect the suggestions and use them to make simple, positive messages. Put a new message into the pocket every day.

Activity four – turn it around

- On a flip chart, draw a circle and add a sad mouth to make a face. Now draw eight lines extending from it. This is sad Spider.

- Ask the children to give you eight suggestions for sad 'hurts' that are making Spider unhappy. For example, 'Someone called me names today'.

- When you have written one sadness along each of the eight legs, turn the sheet of paper round so that there is a happy mouth in the circle. Draw large petal shapes around the leg lines to make a flower.

- Now write a 'kind' sentence into each petal. For example, 'Andy let me join in his game at playtime'. Tell the children that they have the power to 'turn around' another person's sadness. They can do this with acts of kindness.

Activity five – the feelings hat

- Coloured paper hats can be used for quick and easy games that will help to develop emotional intelligence. Use the colours to signify a feeling, just like Moppy!

YELLOW =	HAPPY	BLUE =	SAD
RED =	ANGRY	PALE GREEN =	CALM
WHITE =	AFRAID	ORANGE =	EXCITED

Variations of the feelings hat game:
Model and mirror

- Put on a coloured hat and model the body language and facial expression appropriate to the feeling it signifies. Ask the children to name the emotion that you are modelling. Volunteers can wear the hat and mirror your behaviour.

Why do I feel?

- Young children can usually offer external causes for emotions. However, they can benefit from trying to suggest internal causes. With care, you can support them and show how it is done.

'When I wear the blue hat I am feeling sad. I am quiet and want to be on my own. What could have happened to make me put on the blue hat?'

Matching feelings

- This activity will help children to empathise with the emotions of others. Choose a coloured hat and offer a reason for wearing it.

'I'm wearing the blue hat because [insert a reason]. Who would like to put on another blue hat and finish the sentence, 'I feel like wearing the blue hat today because...'?

Change the emotion

- Wear the blue hat and explain that you must be feeling sad. Invite another child to choose another coloured hat/feeling and suggest what might happen to make you change to that feeling.

◄ For the 'turn it around' activity you will need...

- A flip chart or a large sheet of paper.

- A felt marker pen.

◄ For the ' feelings hat' activity you will need...

- A variety of hats in the following colours: yellow, blue, red, pale green, white and orange. You could also make paper hats from coloured sugar paper.

Sometimes we are ...

circle time session

Use the five steps
of circle time
to explore the
emotion of anger

What you need

• A copy of the book
  Moppy is Angry.

• Small stick-on badges in
  the shape of clouds,
  coloured pale green for
  calm.

Moppy is Angry

Moppy is at a loose end
now that David is at school.
Left at home, he can't think
of anything that he feels like
doing.

Moppy tries a few attention-
seeking tricks such as
pulling faces and shouting
the rudest word he knows
– with little effect. His
frustration becomes anger,
and soon Moppy has turned
bright red! Things get worse
when Moppy is mistaken for
a rug and thrown away with
the rubbish...

The text in italics suggests a script for the
circle time leader to follow.

Meeting Up

• Sit the children in an inward facing circle. Ask everybody to stand up.
  Make eye contact with a child and then smile. The child should smile back.
  Walk towards them and take their place. The object of the game is for
  the child to have moved away before the place is claimed. Continue until
  everybody has had a turn.

Warming Up

• Using the speaking object (see page 4), ask the children if any of them
  would like to share how the smile made them feel: 'A friendly smile
  makes me feel…'

Opening Up

• Tell the children that you are now going to make a very different face.
  Choose a few children who you know to be resilient, and look angrily at
  them. Ask them to share the way your angry face made them feel. Can
  they share their angry faces with the group? Can anyone demonstrate
  how angry people sit and move? (You might need to make sure children
  react with safety in mind!)

• Tell the children that you have a story about a little alien who got
  into a terrible temper that made him do some very silly things. Read
  the story *Moppy is Angry*. Talk about the events in the story and ask
  the children to contribute their own experiences of angry behaviour.
  Explain that everyone feels angry sometimes and then explore how
  Moppy had a choice about how to handle his frustration and anger.

  What happened to make Moppy angry?
  What colour did he become when he was angry?
  What did he do when he was feeling angry?
  What happened because he did those angry things?

Cheering Up

• Ask the children to nominate those who are a calm presence in the
  classroom. Ask these children to come to the front and take a bow.
  Present them with a stick-on badge made in the shape of a cloud from
  pale green card.

angry

calming down

- Tell the children that you know a few techniques to stop anger getting out of control and that you find them very useful sometimes. You are now going to demonstrate these techniques.

    'Take a deep breath while tightening each part of the body until you are "frozen solid". Now you can "thaw" by relaxing each part of your body and allowing your anger to melt away.'
    'Take a deep breath while counting to five. Now count back to one, breathing out slowly.'

Extension activities

Use these activities for follow-up sessions with your class. 'Pass the emotion' is a good choice at the end of your circle time meeting.

STRATEGIES FOR CONTROLLING ANGER

- Anger is a difficult emotion. If we are to help prevent uncontrolled anger forming in the classroom, then we need to integrate a few strategies into daily classroom life.

    Ensure that every child feels that she is a valuable member of your class.
    Provide a safe, responsive, predictable environment.
    Be fair, supportive, firm and consistent: never ridicule a child.
    Watch out for appropriate behaviour and praise it.
    Teach social problem-solving skills.

- Make clear rules for your room. You can use the Golden Rules which are part of Jenny Mosley's Quality Circle Time model:

    We listen to people, we do not interrupt.
    We are honest, we do not cover up the truth.
    We are kind and helpful, we do not hurt other people's feelings.
    We are gentle, we do not hurt anybody.
    We try to work hard, we do not waste time.
    We look after property, we do not waste or damage things.

- If a child is out-of-control, provide a quiet place for calming down.

- Help the children to acquire a vocabulary of 'feeling' words. Use these words to help children to recognise emotion in others.

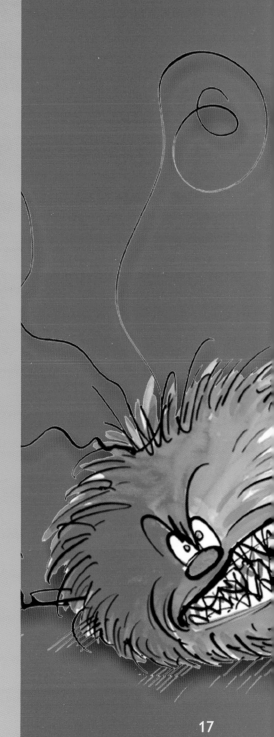

• Listen, reflect and validate without judgement the feelings that a child expresses.

• Encourage children to accept responsibility for their anger. Show them how we ask ourselves questions such as: 'Did I say something that might have upset someone else?' or 'What should I do to make things better?'

• Help children to understand that they can choose how to react when they feel angry. Teach them positive ways to cope with anger such as:

Stop and take a deep breath.
Say what's wrong.
Say what you would like to happen.

• Another version of this strategy is the ABC of anger, suitable for older children:

A is for the ACTUAL BEHAVIOUR that irritates you. For example: 'I don't like it when you shout at me…'
B is for BE HUMAN: say how you are feeling. For example, 'It makes me feel angry.'
C is for the CHANGE that you would like to happen. For example, 'Please keep your voice calm when you speak to me.'

Activity one – storytime/word work

• Tell the children that you will be collecting 'angry words' for the noticeboard. Ask them to tell you about such words that they find in their storybooks.

• Display words that describe anger: rage, wrath, annoy, kick, fierce and so on. Use big red letters. For older children you may want to separate them into 'angry verbs' and 'angry nouns'.

Activity two – storytime display

• Give each child a piece of plain paper and their current reading book. Ask them to find a sentence that describes a character's anger. They will find sentences like this:

'Mad with rage, the evil queen called for her woodsman and told him to take Snow White into the forest.'

• Write the sentence at the bottom of a sheet of paper and ask the child to illustrate it. Add the name of the story and page number on the paper. Display the pictures in the book corner so that other children can spot the sentence when they read the story. Soon you will have a wonderful display of angry behaviour/body language.

For the 'storytime ▶ display' activity you will need…

• Storybooks that include a character experiencing anger.

- Some of your sentences and pictures will show how uncontrolled anger affects other people. Show the children that in some of your sentences angry words can be used to hurt another person. It is useful for children to know that words like 'stupid' and 'ugly' tell us a lot about a person's anger and are said to hurt rather than to give an honest assessment of someone's intelligence or appearance.

Activity three – describing anger

- Ask the children to note any interesting ways in which they hear anger being described. Give them time to copy the sentences and draw pictures of the appropriate characters. Use these to make a wall display.

Activity four – pass the emotion

- Put six coloured cards into a bag, to signify the following emotions:

YELLOW =	HAPPY	BLUE =	SAD
RED =	ANGRY	PALE GREEN =	CALM
WHITE =	AFRAID	ORANGE =	EXCITED

- Pass the bag around the group in your circle meeting. Use the rhyme: 'Round you go, round you go, what emotion will you show?'

- The child who is holding the bag when the rhyme stops must take one coloured card and put it face down on the floor so that nobody else can see. They show the rest of the class the appropriate behaviour and expression for the emotion. The other children then guess the colour of the card that was removed from the bag. If you have been using the Moppy books you may like to use fluffy coloured balls instead of cards. (Let the shy children 'pass' on this activity if they wish.) 'Pass the emotion' is a good activity at the end of your circle time meeting. It offers the chance to explore how moods change with a version of 'pass the parcel'.

◀ for the 'pass the emotion' activity you will need...

- A cloth bag.
- Six small cards in the following colours: red, pale green, yellow, blue, orange and white.

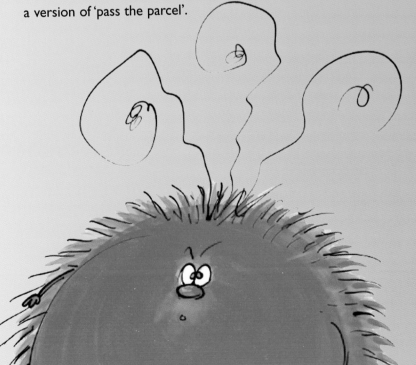

19

Sometimes we are .

Circle time session

The text in italics suggests a script for the circle time leader to follow.

Use the five steps of circle time to explore feelings of calm

You will need

• Some blank cards.
• A copy of *Moppy is Calm*.

Moppy is calm

One morning, things go wrong for Moppy. David and the family try their best to help, but the little alien is a glowing mess of frustration.

Moppy tries all sorts of ways to find calm again, from deep breathing to a spot of exercise… but what made him so cross in the first place?

Meeting up

• Begin with a game of 'Pass the greeting'. Put your hands together and bow toward the child sitting next to you. Ask them to pass the greeting to the next person and so on until it is returned to you.

Warming up

• Using the speaking object ask each child to complete the sentence, 'It makes me feel peaceful and calm when…' (for example: hear the waves on the beach, snuggle up on the sofa, stroke my pet, hold someone's hand). Take a note of these for use in the 'opening up' stage of the session.

Opening up

• This step will introduce the opportunity for the children to talk about their frustrations, and ways of finding a sense of calm. Put the children into small groups and give each group a card with one of the suggestions you have collected from the round in the 'warming up' phase.

• Now ask each group to make up a one-minute play that begins with someone feeling a little bit upset, but which ends with the way of calming down shown on the card. If the card says 'stroking a pet' then the group might make up a play about everyone getting worried and upset when a cat becomes stuck up a tree, and then show what happened to get it down. The play would end with a character stroking their pet and feeling calm again. The plays should focus on what makes the children frustrated and how they find solutions for calm.

• Ask for volunteers to show their plays to the rest of the group in the middle of the circle space. After each play, ask some simple 'trigger' questions. Did they feel calm when they were acting calm? Ask them, when they are in character, to describe how their upset feelings affected them physically (hot, scratchy, jiggly etc) and emotionally (anxious, cross, scared). This will help them to consolidate their awareness of their emotions and gives them the vocabulary to describe them. Write key words on a wall chart so that you have a class collection of descriptive words.

20

Calm

- Pass a gift of calm around the circle.

  'Now let's pass some calm around the circle and then we will all feel calm and peaceful. Sit comfortably on your chair. Put your hands on your lap, palms up. Sigh deeply and slowly. Smile contentedly at the person next to you and ask them to pass on the calm to the person next to them.'

- Read the story *Moppy is Calm* and praise the children for listening quietly and calmly.

Calming down

- Use the following script to share a calming technique.

  'When we need to calm down, the first thing that we do is stop what we are doing and concentrate on making our body and mind peaceful and still. I call this "stop, flop and drop."

  'Curl up your toes until they feel tight and scrunched up. Scrunch up your knees and elbows until you have scrunched up your body.

  'Now let your feet flop so that they feel loose and sleepy. Relax your whole body in the same way that you scrunched it up. Sit or lie still for a little while and try to let all your thoughts drop out of your brain until it is empty and calm.

  'Now listen to the sounds around you and feel the air on your face and hands. Feel the peace inside you. Feel yourself filling up with peace and quietness. This is the feeling of calm.'

Extension activities

Use these activities for follow-up sessions with your class.

Activity one – keeping Moppy calm

- Photocopy the template of Moppy (see page 35) on to some card, and cut it out. Ask the children to draw around the shape and colour it in. Now encourage them to write 'Moppy is still and calm' under the picture.

- On another piece of paper, the children should draw round the Moppy template a few times, moving the outline slightly each time. You now have a picture of Moppy which looks as if he is moving! Add a caption to the picture: 'Moppy is moving fast'.

- When they are displayed side by side, these pictures are a useful visual cue to explain the essence of calm to the very young.

◀ **For the 'keeping Moppy calm' activity you will need...**

- Card, scissors and the activity sheet from page 35.

Activity two - calm blue sea

- This is a script for an alternative calming technique.

'Who has been to the seaside?

'Breathing is like the waves on the sea. Breathe in slowly and imagine a wave coming up a sandy beach. Breathe out slowly and imagine the waves going back to the sea.

'When you breathe in, feel the cool air in your nose. When you breathe out, feel it warm and calm in your mouth.

'As you breathe out, let all your worries and wriggles wash out to sea, until they are far away in the calm blue ocean.

'Silently, in your mind, say to yourself "*calm blue sea*" and make a picture of the beautiful sea inside your head. Do this every time you feel that you need to calm down. It works every time!'

Activity three - picture postcards

- Holiday postcards often depict calm, peaceful views. The landscapes they portray are quiet and free from activity. Make a collection of postcards, holiday posters or holiday adverts from magazines. Ask the children to look at them and notice the colours, the stillness and the peacefulness of the pictures. Let the children use them as a stimulus for their own pictures of somewhere equally calm and peaceful.

- Tell the children to remember this picture. They can keep it inside their head and think of it whenever they need to calm themselves. It will work even better if they can repeat the magic words 'calm blue sea' over and over at the same time. (This mantra works for many adults too!)

Activity four - winding up, winding down

- Wind up a clockwork toy and show it to the children. Let them watch as it slows down. Explain that sometimes we all get 'wound up' and need to 'wind down': this is called 'calming down'. Ask the children if anyone has ever been told to calm down? Can they tell you about it?

- Organise the children in pairs. Ask them to pretend that they have a big wind-up key on their backs. One step at a time, ask them to plan a little dance that has four parts:
ACT ONE - First, they must wind each other up by turning the key on their partner's back. The key is heavy and difficult to turn!
ACT TWO - Next, they must move in a jerky, mechanical way, just like a robot.
ACT THREE - Now they need to slow their movements gradually until they have wound down. As they wind down, they must let their bodies become more floppy.

▶ For the 'picture postcards' activity you will need...

- Images of holiday destinations that promise peace and quiet.

▶ For the 'winding up, winding down' activity you will need...

- A clockwork toy.

- A piece of music that begins slowly, speeds up and then slows down.

ACT FOUR - Finally, they need to move gradually lower and lower until they are lying on the floor, very still and calm.

- Try putting the dance to music. Share it with another class, or perform it in an assembly.

Activity five - safe in the nest

- Ask the children to curl up quietly on the floor. Read the following story, stopping for action at the appropriate points.

'Safe in the nest, curled up tight, something slept through the warm summer night.

A lady in a red hat [put on the red hat] *came along and said,*

"Little things, little things, what can you be? Wake yourself and let me see!"

Out of the nest popped a crowd of baby dragons. They stomped around looking very cross.

[Children stomp around]

The lady in the red hat said, "Shoo, shoo, go away! Go back to sleep for another day!"'

[The children curl up again.]

- Repeat the action story with a different coloured hat for each feeling. Use the following actions for the children at the appropriate point:

Blue hat/sad: 'Out of the nest came some little elephants, slow and sad, trudging round and hanging their heads.'

Yellow hat/happy: 'Out of the nest came some puppies, wagging their tails and yapping at each other.'

Pale green hat/calm: 'Out of the nest came some cool little cats, lying in the garden and soaking up the sun!'

Orange hat/excited: 'Out of the nest jumped a lot of little frogs, hopping and jumping and playing in the pond.'

White/afraid: 'Out of the nest jumped some little birds, wondering what the noise was and cheeping loud in fright!'

- Finish the session by wearing a rainbow hat showing all the colours, so that the children can choose which feeling to act out. Continue: *'Out of the nest popped a class of little children. Sometimes they were cross and sometimes they were sad and sometimes they were happy... just like you! Let's all shake hands and say 'Hello! I don't want YOU to go!'*

◀ **for the 'safe in the nest' activity you will need...**

- Coloured hats in a variety of colours: red, pale green, yellow, blue, orange and white – and a rainbow hat of all colours.

Sometimes we are .

circle time session

The text in italics suggests a script for the
circle time leader to follow.

**Use the five steps
of circle time to
explore the feeling
of being afraid**

What you need
• A white balloon.

Meeting Up

• Show the children a big 'shiver and shake'. Ask the child next to
  you to pass it on round the circle until it gets back to you.

  *'Does anyone know how we are feeling when we quiver and shake? Yes,
  it's something we do when we are scared. It's natural to feel scared and
  we all feel that way sometimes.*

  *'If I met an enormous dinosaur, for instance, I would feel very scared
  because nobody wants to be a dinosaur's dinner. My fear would give me
  enough energy to run away. Phew!*

  *'But sometimes, fear gets in the way and stops us doing things that
  aren't that scary. Sometimes, a fear gets bigger than it really is. As we
  grow up, we need to work out if a fear is a big, real one or a little, not-
  so-scary one that has got too big for its boots!'*

Warming Up

• Pass the speaking object (see page 4) around the group, and ask the
  children to complete the sentence, 'I get a little bit scared when…'

Opening Up

• Choose a confident child to help demonstrate the game 'Big, bad,
  white balloon'. Tell the child that if you say 'face', then they must
  look at you. If you say 'back', then they must turn away.

• Take a white balloon and blow it up a little way. Call out 'back', and
  then blow it up some more. Now call 'face', and this time let out
  some air. Repeat this a few times. Let other children join in the game.

  *'Some fears are like this big, bad, white balloon. When we turn our backs
  away from a fear and refuse to look it in the eye, it gets bigger and
  bigger. When we turn round and face our fear we can begin to make it
  smaller and smaller until it isn't a big, bad, white balloon anymore. [Let
  the air out of the balloon.] Look, it's a scrunched-up, flat, white balloon
  that can't do anything to hurt us.*
  *'The secret with some fears is to get to know them, but you can't get to
  know something if you won't look at it.*

afraid

'Some people are scared of spiders. They say things like, "They're horrible, big, crawly things that might bite me." That makes the white balloon very big indeed. Look... [Blow up the balloon.]
'But, if they face up to their fear and get to know about spiders they would find out that they are actually very little. The ones in our country never bite. Knowing all that means that the big, bad, white balloon gets smaller and smaller and we don't need to be scared of spiders any more.'

- Ask the children to suggest a common fear, such as the dark. Ask them to give reasons why someone might be afraid of the dark. Collect ways of 'facing the fear' that make it smaller and less powerful.

Cheering up

- Explain that some of the bravest people are the ones who do things even though they are afraid. Can the children tell you of occasions when they were brave?

Calming down

- Play some gentle music. A suitable 'chill-out' CD is ideal – many children like the ones that feature dolphins or familiar sounds. Repeat one of the calming techniques suggested in the chapter 'Sometimes we are angry', or the 'calm blue sea' activity from the chapter 'Sometimes we are calm'.

Extension activities

Use these activities for follow-up sessions with your class. 'If someone told me' is an alternative activity for the development stage of your circle time meeting.

Activity one – bursting balloons

- Each child needs a piece of paper folded into eight sections. Ask the children to draw a balloon in each section. The balloons should get bigger in the first four pictures, and then get smaller in the remaining pictures.

- Now ask the children to draw a fear that somebody might have in each balloon (such as spiders). When all the balloons are complete with a picture, the sheet will show the fear getting bigger and then smaller.

- Make a display of the pictures with the title, 'Fears can get very BIG but they get smaller when we face them and get to know them'.

Activity two – fear-busters

- Photocopy the activity sheet on page 34 which depicts a bedroom featuring a few simple pieces of furniture, and a window.

- Put the children in pairs and then ask them to colour in the picture. Encourage them to put spooky things in their drawings: a ghost at the window, a monster under the bed and so on.

- When the pictures are complete, let each pair of children prepare a fear-busters' plan to share with the rest of the class. They can be as imaginative (and as unrealistic) as they like.

- Now ask the teams to share their picture with the class, explaining how their fear-busters' plan will get rid of the spooks and scary things that they have drawn.

- Children can work in pairs, in groups or individually for this activity. Ask them to choose some scary things (depending on the number in the group) such as a dragon, a ghost or a monster. Use this writing frame to devise ways of making fears smaller:

If I met a...
I would...
And...
And...
Because I am brave.

Activity three – if I met a dragon

- Ask your children to contribute some common fears that they think others might have. (This saves them the indignity of admitting openly that they have fears themselves!) Write the fears on pieces of paper and put them in a container.

- Ask for volunteers to come up and take a piece of paper from the container. They should open it and say:

If someone told me,
'I can't do this
And I couldn't go there'
I'd say, 'Let's look for a way
To make you dare.'

'This piece of paper says [insert fear]. Who has a suggestion for helping someone to be brave about that fear?'

For the 'fear-busters' ▶
activity you will need...

- The photocopiable sheet of a bedroom (see page 34).

For the 'If I met a dragon ▶
activity you will need...

- A canister or container with a removable plastic lid. Make a slot in the lid so that slips of paper can be posted through.

- To give this activity more impact, you can make it a daily event. Take just one fear every day and discuss ways of 'facing it' with the class. You can put the container in an accessible place and allow children to add fears as and when they wish.

Activity five – body language

- Choose a child to leave the group. While they are out of the room, distribute the six coloured feelings cards around the circle:

YELLOW =   HAPPY
BLUE =   SAD
RED =   ANGRY
PALE GREEN =   CALM
WHITE =   AFRAID
ORANGE =   EXCITED

- The chosen children must look at their card and then sit on it. Next, they must make a face and try to sit in a way appropriate to their feelings card. The child who left the group is then asked to rejoin everyone else. She needs to identify who is holding each card and explain how she knows. For example, 'You're holding the red card. I know because you are looking very cross!'

Activity six – under the blanket

- Many fears are unfounded. We respond to them by curling up under a 'blanket' of panic and cannot think clearly about the thing that has made us afraid. As we grow, we need to learn strategies that help us to 'reality test' our fears and cut them down to size.

- Tell the children that they are going to play a game. Ask one child to curl up on the floor in the middle of the circle.

    'Let's pretend that Paul is afraid of dogs.'
    [Cover him with the blanket.]
    'In this pretend game, Paul is so afraid of dogs that he is covered in his blanket of fear and he can't see out.'
    [Ask the children to offer suggestions that might help Paul to overcome his fear by seeing it differently. With each suggestion ask Paul if it might help and ask him to come out from under his blanket bit by bit until he is free and standing up.]
    'That has helped Paul to feel a lot less afraid. Thank you everyone and well done. Paul, you are a brave boy for thinking about your fears.'

- Ask the children to suggest things they might be afraid of and repeat the stages described above.

◀ For the 'body language' activity you will need...

- Small cards in the following colours: red, pale green, yellow, blue, orange and white.

◀ For the 'Under the blanket' activity you will need...

- A small blanket.

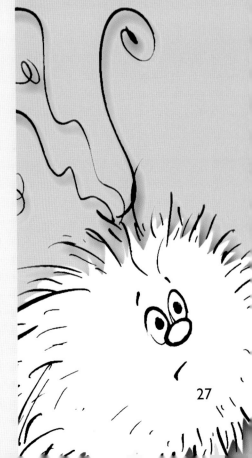

27

Sometimes we are ..

circle time session

The text in italics suggests a script for the circle time leader to follow.

Use the five steps of circle time to explore the feeling of excitement

What you need

- A puppet or a soft toy with floppy arms and legs.

Meeting up

- Sit the children in a circle and ask each child to think of an animal. Soon they will get the chance to move like the animal they have chosen. For instance, they may choose to be a worm and wriggle about, or they may choose to be a frog and hop and jump.

- Now say this rhyme:

The animals are coming to town.
And we are all delighted.
The animals are coming to town
[Point to a child and say their name] …is very excited.

The chosen child must then move about like their chosen animal while the other children try to guess what the animal might be.

'It is certainly exciting when the animals come to town. It doesn't happen very often and that is one thing that makes it exciting. Today we are going to think about how it feels to be excited and about all the things that make us feel excited.'

Warming up

- Passing the speaking object around the group, ask each child to complete the following sentence, 'I was excited when…'

Opening up

- Show the children a puppet or soft toy: try to exaggerate its ability to look listless and floppy!

'Oh dear, Fluffy is looking very floppy today. [Lift Fluffy's arm and let it drop.] He doesn't have any energy, but he's not ill.
'His house is full of toys but he says there is nothing to do. He's just lying on my lap, staring at the ceiling.
'Does anyone have a word for how he might be feeling?
'Yes, bored – that seems like the right word. Are you bored, Fluffy?
'Yes, Fluffy says that he is bored. Have any of you felt like Fluffy? Can you tell us how it feels to be bored? [Let the children share their responses.]

excited

'Well, I can see that boredom is not a nice feeling so it is a good thing that our circle meeting is not about boredom! It is about the opposite feeling. It is about feeling interested and excited. [Make Fluffy sit up sharply.]
'Oh good! Fluffy, I've got your attention now. Let's do a round about the things that make us interested and excited. We'll start with you, Fluffy...
'Well, that's a surprise! Fluffy says that he gets excited when it rains. He likes wet play times because everyone stays in and plays with him. What interests and excites everyone else?'
[Let the children share their responses.]

Cheering up

- Encourage the children to share some of the things that they like doing. Explain that we are all interested and excited by many different things. Read out a list of examples of activities, encouraging the children to clap appropriately for each one: quiet clapping or louder clapping depending on their enthusiasm for the item on the list.

Calming down

- Use the following script as a bridge into the rest of the school day.

'Excitement can be found on grey days if you look for it, so you don't need to be bored or fed-up.

'Excitement is a lovely fizzy feeling that makes us all wiggly and jiggly inside. Sometimes it is difficult to keep excitement under control. When excitement gets out of control it can make us silly and "overexcited" – then we need to remember to calm down.

'We are going to calm down now and think about how special each one of us is.'

- Listen to the gentle rustle of a rainstick or some peaceful music such as Grieg's 'Morning' from the Peer Gynt suite. With their eyes closed and hands in laps, give the children a minute to think about how unique and special they are.

Extension activities

Use these activities for follow-up sessions with your class. 'Pass the parcel' is a good choice at the end of your circle time meeting.

Activity one – look closer

- Read the following verse to the children:

Sometimes, we are not excited and interested.
Sometimes we are BORED.
Sometimes we need to LOOK CLOSER...

- Give the children some mundane, everyday things that are apparently boring – scraps of newsprint, a chipped mug, a large paperclip (anything you have around that you deem suitable!) Ask the children to remember and then write down their first impression of the 'boring' object.

- Give the children a magnifying glass and ask them to have a closer look. Can they describe what they see when they look closer? Ask them to draw 'I looked closer' pictures for the display board.

- Explain how even the most boring situation can become interesting – even exciting – when a person has learned to look closer.

Activity two – use your imagination

- Divide the class into groups and give each group a classroom object. Tell them to look closer at the object and see if they can use their imagination to change the object into something more interesting. A stapler might become a telephone for contacting aliens; a large piece of paper could become a magic carpet. Set them the task of working out how their 'new' object could be used.

- Let the children perform a sixty-second drama to demonstrate the use of their 'new' object. Remind them that the most boring situation can be made interesting and exciting if they remember to use their imagination.

Activity three – grey day

- Excitement and interest can make life seem much more colourful. Fold a piece of paper in two and tell the children to map out an identical line drawing on each side. Ask them to colour one side to make it look boring and to colour the other side to make it look exciting.

- Explain that life is like their picture. They have the power to 'colour' their own lives. They can choose to colour them grey and boring or bright and exciting!

Activity four – boredom buster

- Organise the children into small groups. Give each group a commonplace object, such as a paper clip, peg, empty paper bag, old sports bag or envelope. Tell them to make a list of 'five things we could do with our object'. Ask them to share their ideas with the rest of the class.

For the 'boredom buster' ▶ activity you will need...

- A selection of everyday objects: a stapler, an old mug, a plant pot, a paper bag etc.

- Explain that this activity is a 'boredom buster' that can make even a boring day at home much more exciting. Offer a reward to any children who can come into school and describe boredom busters that they have explored at home.

Activity five – pass the parcel

- Party games are always exciting activities for children. Pass the parcel can be played as a round during circle time. The children will experience the feelings that excitement brings and be able to discuss them.

- Wrap a star in layers of wrapping paper and pass the parcel round the group. Repeat this rhyme as the parcel goes round:

  All of us are different
  No-one is the same
  But everyone's excited
  When we play this party game!

- Each time the rhyme ends, the child who is holding the parcel must tear off a layer of newspaper and finish one of the following sentences. The sentences can be repeated to encourage alternative answers from different children.

  When I am excited, my tummy feels... [insert answer eg wobbly!]
  When I am excited, my head feels... [insert answer eg fizzy!]
  When I am excited I want to... [insert answer eg jump around!]
  The thing that excites me most is... [insert answer eg holidays.]
  On rainy, grey days I stop myself from getting bored by... [insert boredom buster eg listening to music.]

- This can continue until the star is revealed. Write the child's name on the star and they can keep it as a prize.

- Discuss the answers that the children have given you about the ways in which they relieve boredom, and how excitement makes them feel. Key words can be listed on your display boards and the children can draw pictures to illustrate what each word means.

◀ For the 'Pass the parcel' activity you will need
- A gold cardboard star and some wrapping paper.

Managing emotions
Steps to managing behaviour

Young children's feelings can change from one moment to the next. Each emotion can be as much of a surprise to them as it is to you. Often, they can be overwhelmed – in despair one moment, bursting with excitement the next.

As adults we can help children to manage their emotions by providing a positive model. As you build their confidence in dealing with strong emotional states, they are becoming self-managing people.

The first steps involve helping children to deal with two key questions:

- How can I control my feelings?

- How can I show my feelings appropriately?

Listen and respond with understanding

Make sure the child knows that they are understood. Reflect what you suspect she is feeling. For example, you might see Anna wanting to take part in an activity with the others but clearly worried about asking to do so. Ask her directly: is this how she is feeling? If she agrees, acknowledge why she might be feeling like that: 'Yes, it's hard to join in when everyone else has got there first.' Use examples from your own life to show that it's not unusual to feel like this and that the feelings don't last. Suggest an appropriate way for the child to get what she wants.

Give children the language to express themselves

Develop a 'feelings' vocabulary by asking the children to label how they are feeling. You might give them examples: 'Are you feeling a bit sad because playtime's nearly over and you haven't had a chance to join in yet?' Children also need to appreciate that we can feel different things all at once: 'You were excited about coming out to play after working so hard and now you're disappointed.'

Acknowledge and confirm how the child is feeling

You might not think there is a reason for a child to be upset, but it doesn't help to say so! The feeling is real to them. Show that you understand why they might be feeling this way.

Give praise and build confidence: be positive!

Don't let children build up negative beliefs about themselves. If they get into a pattern of thinking 'I can't' then they will not face a situation even if it seems straightforward to you. Show them how: give them hope and confidence so that they can try on their own. Give praise as children learn to understand and then manage their emotions. Let them remember the positive messages, not the negative ones.

Be a role model

Keep aware of how you are reacting to the children. Don't use harsh words even if your temper is at breaking point. Talk about the behaviour, never the child or the affect the behaviour is having on you. 'You're driving me mad' or 'You careless child!' won't help the child to manage their emotions. Show that you can see why they are upset, but that their behaviour isn't going to help. Suggest a way for them to calm down.

Offer a model for dealing with frustrating situations. If a temper is the problem, then show how to check for tension: are fists and tummy tight? Demonstrate how to 'blow the anger out' by breathing deeply.

The children are learning to minimise the strength of their emotions. Remind them that perfection isn't needed. A brave attempt is just as good!

33

Photocopiable activity sheet

Use with the 'fear-busters' activity on page 26

Photocopiable activity sheet

Use with the 'keeping moppy calm' activity on page 21

Collect the whole series
and get to know the lovable
little alien in all his moods!

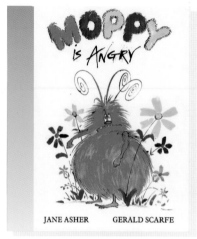

Moppy is Angry
(ISBN 0-9540585-9-3)

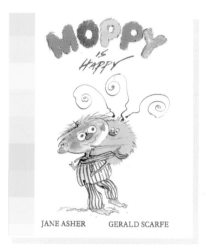

Moppy is Happy
(ISBN 0-9540585-8-5)

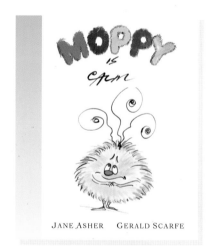

Moppy is Calm
(ISBN 1-9048660-8-5)

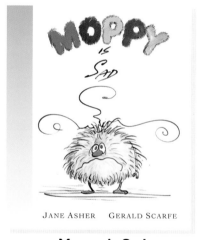

Moppy is Sad
(ISBN 1-9048660-7-7)

For information about training in all aspects of circle time or to order books contact:
Positive Press Ltd, Jenny Mosley Consultancies,
28a Gloucester Road, Trowbridge, Wiltshire BA14 OAA

Tel: 01225 719204 Fax: 01225 755631 E-mail: positivepress@jennymosley.co.uk
www.circle-time.co.uk